Flight
of a
Butterfly

LYNDSEY AUSTIN

FLIGHT OF A BUTTERFLY
ISBN 978-1-913713-11-9
Copyright © Lyndsey Austin

First published 2020 by Compass-Publishing
Edited and typeset by The Book Refinery Ltd
www.thebookrefinery.com

The right of Lyndsey Austin to be identified as the author of this work has been
asserted in accordance with the Copyright,
Designs and Patents Act, 1988.

A CIP catalogue record for this book is available from the
British Library.

Printed and bound by CMP Ltd. Poole, Dorset.

This book is based on a true story.
To protect identities, all names have been changed in this book.
All conversations have been remembered and reproduced to
the best of the author's ability.

Contents

Introduction 9

Part 1 – The Past 13

Chapter One – My childhood.......................................15

Chapter Two – Blinking 19

Chapter Three – Court day...21
Positive thoughts 21

Chapter Four – Feeling unloved 23

Chapter Five – Courage...25

Chapter Six – Court day #2...27

Chapter Seven – Life was better 29

Chapter Eight – 14 going on 20 33

Chapter Nine – My daughters' father 37

Chapter Ten – Violence & drugs = no self-worth 43
The pipe 43
Arrest and court..44

Chapter Eleven – #Metoo 51

    Attempted rape..*51*

    Rape *52*

Chapter Twelve – Street life 57

    Drugs and raving...*57*

Chapter Thirteen – Motherhood................................59

    The hostel...*60*

    Labour *61*

    The beatings *64*

Chapter Fourteen – Wedding bells 67

    The move...*67*

    The wedding *67*

    Growing as a person..*70*

Chapter Fifteen – New relationship...........................75

Chapter Sixteen – Changes 79

    Coming face to face with my dad *81*

Chapter Seventeen – The big 'C' word 83

    The operation *86*

    Scar *87*

Chapter Eighteen – Ibiza, baby!.................................89

Chapter Nineteen – The big 40!..................................91

    Barbados: April 2014..*92*

Chapter Twenty – Wedding bells #2?.........................95

Chapter Twenty-one – Suicidal thoughts 99

Chapter Twenty-two – Personal and
spiritual development.. 103
The random holiday: 2017..105

Chapter Twenty-three – Transformation 107
Getting a coach: January 2019 109
Forgiveness 109

Chapter Twenty-four – Unstoppable.......................... 111

Part 2 – The Future 113

Chapter Twenty-five – Being body-confident............. 115
Confidence-boosting affirmations.....................................116

Chapter Twenty-six – My training.............................. 117
Getting out of your own way! 119
Adversity 119

Chapter Twenty-seven – Self care............................... 123

Chapter Twenty-eight – Miracle mornings! 125
How I start my day...125

Conclusion 127
My mission 130

Acknowledgements... 133

I want to teach every young girl out there who has ever dreamed of a fairytale life that the first, most important person she should fall in love with, is herself.

Introduction

This book is my journey: how I overcame fear, shame and adversity and turned them into my strengths. My story is proof that, if you learn to love and believe in yourself, you can transform your life, as I have. I started writing it three years ago and it's taken me until now to be able to share it with you all.

You read it now in the form of a diary – how I lived it all, and also how I look back on it today; the lessons that I have learnt; how I have healed and what I, as an adult now, would tell my child self. I want you to relate to it and connect to my story – the young girl journeying to womanhood: how we feel and how we, without realising, give to others the love we should give to ourselves.

This book is for all those who have suffered trauma, who have struggled, and who have spent countless nights questioning their self-worth. As I share my experiences with you, I want you to know how much you are worth and that you too can transform your own life. There really is light at the end of the tunnel: a great life out there just waiting for you to live it.

Through reading my story, I want you to realise that you are everything and more. I want you to believe in yourself and to take action – even just that first step.

And I have you. I am holding your hand all the way. I believe in you.

So don't feel shame, but be confident in who you are. You can't expect to find real love if you don't love yourself. You will always be the most important person in your life and you need to look after YOU.

Because you are number one!

I have lived with the fear of my story for years, hiding away the true me and what I have experienced – my many traumas. I felt ashamed, but why should I feel shame? Speaking my truth has set me free. I stepped into my superpower and so can you.

* ✳ Just know you are loved.
* ✳ You are stronger than you think.
* ✳ You have life for a reason.
* ✳ You are beautiful inside and out.
* ✳ You are a badass.
* ✳ You are love.

As you read about my healing and how it happened, I hope you will discover how it can help you. With the benefit of hindsight, I also share what I would say to my younger self, lessons learnt, and a sprinkling of special *'messages to you'* throughout the book. Read these carefully. I've got the advantage of 20/20 vision!

Remember, you've got you. You are the driver of your life, so put your foot on the gas and let's go!

With
broken wings,
she learnt
to fly.

- Karen K Sandhu

Part 1

The Past

Chapter One

My childhood

My mum married my dad when she was 20. He was the first man she had ever had a sexual relationship with. She gave birth to my sister first, then, 11 months later to me.

My childhood wasn't great at all. I do have some nice memories but not many. My dad was very violent towards my mum. One night, I recall how she just left in her nightwear, leaving my sister and me with my dad. That was my first really bad memory. In the morning, I asked my dad why she had gone. I remember being half asleep in the night and hearing shouting. Dad didn't answer me. I knew my mum had left because she was scared, but I remember feeling confused.

When Christmas day arrived, Mum had been gone for a few weeks and I had no idea where she was.

'Happy Christmas, kids,' Dad said that morning. 'Oh, and your mother's coming for dinner today.'

Mum arrived and there was tension. As young as I was, I could still feel it. I remember us eating and then Dad started talking to my mum in a nasty manner. His voice got louder. Then, suddenly, he stabbed her in the face with a fork.

My sister and I froze. My mum was crying and her face was bleeding from the wound. I could see the fear there and I really didn't know what to think. Dad shouted, 'Get out!' and Mum just ran out of the house with her head down.

'Sorry, girls,' I heard her say.

From then on, my childhood was always upsetting. Within weeks, my dad was flirting with two ladies who lived across the road. They were very attractive women. My sister and I used to play with their daughters. Nothing came of that but then, within a few weeks, Dad moved into a house around the corner my sister and me. He'd been having a relationship with a woman there. She had two children, a boy and a girl. And that was where we lived for five years.

The woman wasn't nice to me or my sister. I started bed-wetting. I missed my mum so much and I'd cry at night, not wanting to be in the house. My dad would give me a good beating every time I wet the bed. I was so scared of him and I dreaded every morning. Waking up, I'd look to see if my bed was wet, afraid of what was to come. The woman's son used to call me 'piss-the-bed' at school. He would tell my friends about it. I just felt shame. I was only seven years old.

Both my sister and I had long brown hair. Dad's new girlfriend cut it short. 'Why has she done this to us?' was all I could think at the time. Now I look back, I understand that she wanted to take away our beauty. She also used to make our clothes: long dresses with flowers all over as I remember. I had big clumpy shoes too, as I was heavy on my feet, and she had metal caps put on the heels because I'd wear them down so quickly. You could hear me coming and the other kids at school always laughed.

My mum used to see us as often as she could. We'd see her for an hour here and there. Welfare was different in those days. It was hard to see your children. We had a welfare officer called Mrs Kennedy. I'll get to her soon.

One Christmas, my mum gave my sister and me twin prams. It was the best thing ever as we had nothing. Dad's girlfriend sold them so she could get her living room decorated. She just sat there and smiled and said, 'Well, my living room needs decorating.'

I was still bed-wetting. It really was crazy how I used to dream about being on the toilet. One morning, I hid the wet bed with my blanket. When I came home from school, I was scared. I walked through the door and Dad's girlfriend shouted, 'Go to your room!'

I shared the bedroom with my sister and Dad's girlfriend's daughter. I had the bottom bunk bed. The woman shouted at me, 'You've wet the bed again, you dirty little bitch!' and her son was calling me 'piss-the-bed' again.

I went and sat in the bedroom, dreading my dad coming home. Then there was a knock on the front door. It was a boy I really liked. I'll never forget him. He was my first ever playground crush. He was blond with blue eyes and all the girls liked him. I was thinking, 'Please don't let Dad's girlfriend's son answer the door.' But, yes, he answered, and he told my crush I'd wet the bed.

A few minutes later, I heard stones being thrown at my bedroom window. I went over to see who it was and there was my crush. He had climbed up the tree and was calling me 'piss-the-bed' and laughing at me. I fell on the floor, crying and thinking, 'How am I going to face him now? How am I going to face everyone at school?' It was all such a mess.

A few hours later, in came my dad. I was lying there in fear as I heard him come into my room. He pulled back the blanket, then, slap, slap, slap! 'You dirty piss-the-bed,' he said. The pain was so bad and I had big hand prints on my butt and the top of my legs.

What I would tell my younger self about this...

Lessons learnt:

How people treat you is a reflection of themselves. My father was miserable and selfish. He took his frustration out on me as I was always closer to my mother, which you'll learn later on in this book. He obviously had no clue how to raise two girls, especially two girls he had traumatised. My bed-wetting was a cry for help. I was scared and I was alone. I had no mother figure to fall back on. However, I vowed to myself from this point forward that, should I ever have children, I would never treat them this way.

Chapter Two

Blinking

It was a nervous habit. My eyes would just blink all the time.

One day I came in from school. I was standing there, listening to my dad telling me the chores I had to do. The next minute, he'd smacked me so hard across my face because of my nervous blink. There it was again: a hand print. And it was the same every time he caught me blinking. 'Stop doing that, you stupid prat,' he would say.

I was frightened all the time. One thing that still sticks in my head is how his girlfriend used to take the light bulb out of the landing light at night. I would just lie awake in bed, scared of the dark. That filled me with so much fear. I still sleep with the light on, even now.

Mrs Kennedy was my and my sister's welfare officer. She had long red hair and such a warm, beautiful smile. She was such a caring lady too and, as our welfare officer, she used to come and see us once a week. She would bring us treats and ask us how we were. I always said I was ok, of course, but I wasn't. Inside I was so unhappy.

Then, one day, I found the courage to tell Mrs Kennedy how I really felt. I always remember her saying she was here to help and there would be a process she'd have to take. There must have already been talks going on that I was unaware of as, by this time, my mum wanted full custody of my sister and me. I cried for my mum so much and I always felt empty inside.

What I would tell my younger self about this...

Lessons learnt:

Speaking up is always the right thing to do. Had I not spoken up to Mrs Kennedy at this time, I may have had to continue living with my father. The historian, Thucydides wrote, 'The secret to happiness is freedom, and the secret to freedom is courage.' All it takes is one conversation with someone you trust to change the direction your life is going in.

Chapter Three

Court day

I was dreading it. I was eight years of age now. Dad came back from court that day.

'Yes, girls,' he said to my sister and me, 'your mum, the witch, has lost the case. I have full custody of you both.'

My heart sank; my sister just looked at me. Dad had more of an emotional control over my sister. He used to play on her emotions, saying how he couldn't live without us.

Each day, I just felt more and more empty. I felt like this was it. I was trapped with him forever.

Positive thoughts

When I think back to this and what I know now, I relate to the secret and the law of attraction. My sister and I used to play in an empty car park. I had a piece of white chalk and I drew on the ground the plan of a house I dreamed of living in. I drew four bedrooms, a big living room, kitchen, bathrooms, a big garden and a drive. I even drew my sofas and beds, the bath, the sink, tables, lamps. I would sit there on my sofa drawn on the concrete, just like this really was my house. I'd walk into a room, visualising the décor and the beautiful furniture. It was my safe, happy house.

I went back to the car park day after day, to sit on the sofa in my dream; in my vision on a concrete floor. I would say out loud, 'I'm going to be happy and live in a house like this with my husband and children, and I'm going to be the happiest person ever.'

At the age of 30, I still had that dream. You'll read about it later in this book.

What I would tell my younger self about this...

Lessons learnt:

Our beliefs as children shape our minds as we become adults. At the time, this visualisation was simply a way to escape from my bleak reality. However, just pretending, even for a little while, was one of the best coping mechanisms for me, and I've carried it forward into my adult life. I would tell that little girl now, 'Keep dreaming, for you don't know what you've just created in the future.'

Chapter Four

Feeling unloved

Months went by. Everything stayed the same. Going to bed hungry, with no cuddles, was just life.

My stepmother had this big wooden spoon that used to hang on the kitchen wall. It was a dark wood and huge. One day, I was so hungry I cut a big slice of banana cake that she'd baked. She went crazy and lined us all up, me, my sister and her own two children. Those two were laughing, of course, even though they'd gone along with it.

My stepmother shouted, 'Who's has been eating the cake?'

I was so scared, I admitted it. And, smack, smack, smack – she hit me so hard with this large wooden spoon across my legs. My sister just stood there, looking on in fear as the other two smirked.

My stepmother had a cat called Beauty, who got ill and was dying. She got us all standing and praying for her cat. I stood in silence. I didn't really care for the cat. Her son would hiss at it and tell it to go and get me. The cat would pounce on me and claw me. I just couldn't show love for something else I was frightened of. And because I just stood there, not crying, I got a slap round the head. There was always something.

What I would tell my younger self about this...

Lessons learnt:

Looking back now, I can see this is how a lot of relationships in my childhood went. I couldn't show love for something I had fear of, my father included. The beatings did nothing but make me stronger; I became numb to them. Imagine beating a child for being hungry? A child you are supposed to care for? A child who is your responsibility? I was always an honest child, and even now I will tell my own children that honesty is the best policy. I took the beating for eating some cake. It wasn't deserved. However, I was true to myself and did not let my sister or step-siblings take the wrath for my decision.

Chapter Five

Courage

There were days my sister and I would walk home from school and my mum would be hiding in the bushes on our route back. She would be with my Auntie B, reaching out to give us treats, chocolates and sweets. I said to my mum, 'I'm going to tell Mrs Kennedy that I want to live with you.'

That's when I finally got the courage.

Welfare had to have a meeting. It had to go back to court and through the months ahead, my dad made my life hell. He didn't speak to me. I was still wetting the bed and being hit for doing so. I would pray to God, 'Please let me go and be with my mum.' I begged my sister to pray for the same thing, but by this time Dad had fully brainwashed her to stay with him; to believe that he needed her; that he couldn't go on if she left him.

What I would tell my younger self about this...

Lessons learnt:

My father resented me for wanting to live with my mother. He always knew this was what I wanted and he took it out on me from the moment she left. I wasn't susceptible to his gaslighting and he knew this too. I'm so glad I prayed to live with my mother, for I fear the person I would have become had I fallen victim to my father's words.

Chapter Six

Court day #2

The day of the hearing arrived. No one was talking to me. I went out to play down at the waste ground and on one of the train tracks. That's what we did back then. So dangerous!

I was walking home around 4pm and I saw my dad get out of his car in his suit. He spotted me.

'Get here,' he said. 'You're going.'

My sister was in the house. She was standing there, crying. My dad got a bin bag; put all my belongings in it. 'You're going,' he said, while my sister was begging me, 'Please don't leave me, please, please...' I was so upset. I wanted her to come with me but she was under the power of my dad and that was that.

He dropped me outside my Auntie B's house. Just me and my bin bag. I was left there, waiting for my mum, who wasn't back from court yet. As she didn't drive, she was still on the bus journey. That's how quick he got me out.

I was now ten years old and I remember thinking, 'Now I'm free from him.'

What I would tell my younger self about this...

Lessons learnt:

My father couldn't cope with the fact that he had lost control of me; that he couldn't bully me anymore; couldn't take his anger and frustration out on me anymore. Looking back now, I can see this was a major turning point in my life, for this was the new home life where I would finally be happy.

Chapter Seven

Life was better

My mum and I lived with my Auntie B. I was so happy there, the happiest I had ever been. Mum then managed to get a bungalow, and for the first time, I had a bedroom to myself. My stepdad, who is so kind and loving, decorated it all in a Barbie theme for me. There were two single beds in it as my mum was ever hopeful that, one day, my sister would come and live with us. We still went to the same primary school so I continued to see her every day, and she'd come and stay the odd weekend. But I'm sad to say we did lose the bond that we had. I believe it was because we didn't live together. I'm also ashamed to admit that, despite his loving efforts, I could be quite difficult for my stepfather. I wasn't used to such love at this point. It all felt alien.

What I would tell my younger self about this...

Lessons learnt:

This was a crucial turning point in my adolescent years as I finally felt loved. I was in a loving home, with my wonderful mother and a kind and gentle stepfather. This was the family I had always dreamed of. I often look back on those days and wonder, if things had played out differently, would my relationship with my sister be different? Would we have been closer?

Teenage Years

The greater the storm, the brighter your rainbow.

- Karen K Sandhu

Chapter Eight

14 going on 20

Secondary school was hard for me as I had warts come up on my hands, then one on the side of my face. I got bullied for it. Girls would call me 'Winnie the witch'. This damaged my perception of myself. I tried everything: if I cut it out from my face, it would just get bigger and having people stare wasn't nice. Name-calling would fill me with this fear. I felt so ugly and I used to dread going to school.

In the end, I went to see a specialist. It was a slow process of having the warts frozen, which caused swelling and brought more attention. The comments carried on. I just used to put my head down and cry secretly inside. I literally felt like an ugly witch. It took a few months for them to finally go and the bullying did ease off. Bullies always find someone else, don't they?

My mum wanted me to take up a hobby. I thought, why not dance? I'd always had a love for music and dance – I suppose it's mostly every young girl's dream, right? So I went to a dance school called the Sylvia Bird School of

Dance. I did all my exams in tap, ballet and modern and I loved dancing! I performed in a few shows and felt like I'd found myself in the movements and had a purpose.

That's where I met some great friends. As you do, a few years later, we began to drink underage together, and I even went to the wrong school to be with one of them sometimes! How was that even allowed?! We still ask ourselves that now when we meet for a catch-up. More on that shortly.

I had a few jobs from the age of 13, waitressing and retail Saturday work. I loved the feeling of being able to treat myself. And that's when it all started to go a little crazy. I went off the rails and would wag school. My mum caught me in town once. I ran off and when I got home later I said, 'No, Mum, you were seeing things!' As a result, I didn't do very well in my exams. I did, however, receive an A in Art and Dance. I loved to draw and dance. I used to dance to Irene Cara, 'What a Feeling', and I adored being in that moment. There's something about music that makes you feel so free; like you can express yourself through your movements. I didn't get Maths or English, though, which is why I'm surprised I'm writing this book!

My good girlfriend from dancing and I would go out on a Wednesday night up to town, drinking and flirting around the footballers who played for the first team. I was 15 and getting into clubs. Then, the next day, I'd go to my friend's school, not mine, and I'd sit in her lessons! How it happened, I'll never understand, even when I look back on it, but I actually ended up going on a holiday to Spain with my friend's school, and that was a story to tell. All the girls and lads would wait till the teachers were asleep, then go out clubbing. And we'd be in and out of each other's rooms.

We did get taught a lesson one night, when we all decided to go and swim in the sea, drunk. As we chatted, we drifted further and further out, until one of the lads said, 'Look how far we've floated out to sea!' There were six of us. We did manage to stay calm and get back to shore but, gosh, we were lucky. God must have been watching over us all.

I think I behaved like this because my mum tried to give me everything in those five years with her – or perhaps I was just messed up from how my dad had treated me. Either way, I was being a rebellious teenager, drinking and not really caring about anything.

What I would tell my younger self about this...

Lessons learnt:

I used my adolescent years as a reason to act up for all the injustice I felt I'd received in my life leading to this point. I'd been angry at the world for so long; angry at the bullies at my own school. Maybe I was even angry with myself to some extent? I bet that if I'd sat my GCSEs at my friend's school, I may even have got good grades with the amount of time I spent there!

Your teen years are the years you make mistakes: the years you look back on in the future and find yourself laughing at in disbelief. I have some very dark memories of my teen years. However, the bullying helped me develop the thick skin I have today.

Chapter Nine

My daughters' father

I was 15 years old when I met my daughters' father. I used to babysit for a lady who had two mixed-race boys, and he used to come round there and chat to me and my friend. He was tall, 5 foot 11, with dreadlocks. He was also very good looking and funny. When I look back, that's how he got me, I guess, with his looks and charm. I was so wrong about him.

He was 24. He was my boyfriend. And in a way, he was the father figure I'd been so desperately seeking.

And I ran away from home.

At that time, I'd met a friend who I'm still close with today. I had no job and she wasn't earning any money either. We joke about it now, but we basically lived on bread and cheese spread. I would have my boyfriend, T to stay with me at hers. I felt loved but it wasn't love, for how could I know what real love was? I felt I had to impress this guy – almost perform in an effort to receive his attention. And that's where it all started.

His brother was a pimp and T followed in his footsteps. Older than T, and taller, his brother was a really strong character. He actually got shot dead years later and, to this day, the murderer has never been found. His girlfriend worked the beat in our local red-light area as a prostitute. She used to steal money from clients too, which is where it began for me.

Picture this: one morning, T and I were in bed at my friend's house when T's brother came banging at the door, shouting, 'Open up, quick!'

T raced to let him in and his brother came rushing past him saying that his girlfriend, S had called the police.

He looked at me and said, 'Lyndsey, I have a shotgun in the flat.' He had a hand on each of my shoulders and he was looking right in my face, towering over me. He said, 'You need to go and get the gun and bring it here.'

I looked at T. He replied, 'Just go quick. You'll be ok.'

Their flat was literally two minutes away. I put my shoes on and ran over there. When I banged on the door, S came to answer. I asked her what had happened and she ranted at me, saying T's brother had gone to hit her like he always did. So she'd called the police and told them there was a shotgun in the flat. But now she was panicking.

'Quick,' she said to me, 'put on my mac and hold the gun inside it so no one will see it when you leave.'

I went out of the front door with the shotgun and closed it behind me. But when I looked up to my left, through the door leading to the lift I could see policemen lined up against the wall the whole way down. I could see their handguns against the sides of their heads. They were wearing bulletproof vests and caps, their faces so serious as they looked at me.

In that moment, I froze, kicked on the door and shouted, 'S!' Instantly, she answered. I barged in and yelled, 'Run! The police!' And as quick as that, S grabbed the shotgun and threw it out onto the balcony. A split second after that, the police came rushing in.

One of the officers knew S and asked her where T's brother was. She said she'd called the police and had lied about there being a shotgun. They asked me who I was and I told them I was just a friend. As four officers looked around the flat, my heart was pounding. They were looking in every room and I was dreading them opening the balcony door. I could see out of the window that they'd taped off the entrance to the block, and officers were standing there with guns.

As one officer went towards the balcony, S said, 'You're not listening. I was lying.' And at that point, the officer said he was taking her in for wasting police time. So S said she thought there had been a gun and had panicked. I learnt in the years to come that she knew how to blag anyone.

When the police left, I just sat there and couldn't believe what had happened. S called me a gangster girl – and it kind of made me feel that I was.

I returned to my friend's house. T and his brother were pleased with the outcome, which, as crazy as it seems meant to me that I felt I'd shown T I loved him. And I thought doing what he wanted me to do would prove to him that I was 'worth it'. Ridiculous when I look back now, but be mindful, I was only 15.

That's when he started buying me clothes to make me feel like he was spoiling me. He bought me some pink trainers and a pink tracksuit and that was it. I was off, standing on the corner on the beat. I was a prostitute at 15. Did I know any different? No. I thought that was love. I was with a man just like my father, thinking that was love.

I would hit the beat after 12 midnight, as the police would be out before then looking for young groomed street workers. And that was me, having sex with strangers: £15 in the car and £20 in a flat. There was a local lady who used to charge us £3 a time to use a room at her flat – crazy.

The first time I ever solicited myself was in a car. I was tensed up. I could feel myself shaking and crying inside. The guy sensed it and dropped me back to my corner. I think he felt sorry for me. (Trust me, it could have been a lot worse – and violent, as it did get. We'll get to that.)

There was one time I'll never forget. I was sitting on the wall on the beat and my mum came and sat next to me. She was begging me, crying, 'Please, please come home...' I just got up and ran. All I cared about was T and wanting to be with him. I never gave a thought for my mother. I was brainwashed and in love with him: my children's father. My abuser. The police soon began to notice me as, by this time, I was out on the streets selling myself in the day. They knew who I was and would take me to my mum's. But I'd just run back to T.

What I would tell my younger self about this...

Lessons learnt:

At this time, I let my love for T overpower my rational thoughts. I believed that in order to prove myself to him, I had to do whatever he wanted. I believed that would make him love me more. I often reflect on this part of my life and want to cuddle the 15-year-old me. She didn't have to do any of that. She was worthy of a greater love; she just didn't know it yet.

Chapter Ten

Violence & drugs = no self-worth

When I was working on the beat, I was expected to take back £100 every night or day I was out. I was scared the police would see me. I felt shame, knowing that my mum knew what I was doing, but the control T had over me and the power of my love for him were stronger. One night, I went home with only £80. And that was the first beating. I felt the slap across my face, then he dragged me around the flat by my hair, kicking me in the face, ribs, everywhere. The first slap felt like my dad. Then they got harder.

The pipe

Drugs: I'll never forget my first crack pipe. The hit was a high that made me feel numb inside, and that's what I wanted to feel. I wanted something to take over my pain. Every night after work, T and I would smoke it. The crack would block out all the pain of selling my body and being beaten up. That was now me hooked, making money for us both to smoke crack. And when there wasn't enough, I started stealing money off my clients. I was now street-robbing; anything to please this man. This monster.

I was losing weight rapidly. I'd gone down to a size 4–6 and looked like a bag of bones – a real life Olive Oyl from *Popeye*. I wasn't eating or sleeping much. Life was all about street-working then crack to numb me, and all the time I thought I was doing what I had to do to get T to love me.

One night I took a punter (that's what we called them) up to the flat where we lived. T came in and made out like he'd caught me out, as if he didn't know I was a prostitute. He gave the man some punches in his face, and the man was petrified. He begged, 'Please let me go – I have a family...' I took everything out of his pockets. There was £1000 in there. That was the man's wages to give to his staff. At the time I didn't care and neither did T. We just took his money, then let him go. I'll never forget the fear in his face and, as I write this, I really hope he forgave me.

That night and into the next day, we spent it all on crack cocaine.

Arrest and court

Yes, it finally happened. I was out street-working one night when I saw the police. I managed to run off as I was getting good on my feet. As always, when I got back to the flat, T and I smoked crack. But he'd be so paranoid over every noise.

'Be quiet!' he hissed at me suddenly. He could hear someone outside.

Then there was banging on the door. It was the police.

As quick as a flash, T hid the crack and acid tablets he had in the air vent. I then opened the door to be greeted with, 'We're arresting you both for theft...'

This was for robbing the man of his £1000.

In 1989, I appeared in juvenile court for the theft and prostitution. I took all the blame. I had to otherwise T would have gone to prison. I made out that I'd been set up by a man who'd come into the flat, masked up, and forced me to steal from the punter. T never got charged, but the police and the punter knew the truth, of course. And it was all down to evidence: my word against the victim's. My fear of T would always win. He would have beat me hard if I'd pointed the finger at him. I'd be known as a 'grass' as we used to say back then.

I stood in the dock. Said my name and age: 'I'm Lyndsey Austin. I'm 16 years old.' Then I glanced up and saw my dad; saw the look of hate in his face. I looked at the judge and I felt fearful and confused, panic going right through my body. I felt so scared, like that scared little girl again.

The judge asked what my plea was. I said, 'Guilty.' And he made me feel so small. He was right to do so really. The victim was a family man and I'd taken from him. I was ordered to pay all the money back and to get a job to do this. I was also given a two-year probation order. As soon as the hearing was finished, I ran out of court. I didn't even look back for the fear of seeing my dad. T thought it was great that I never grassed him up. A 'ride-or-die chick' he called me. I'm glad I never got the tattoo...

Heroin was the next thing I did. I only did it a few times and I thank God now for protecting me more against this. I would take it with, S, T's brother's girlfriend.

One day I was at hers. She was staying in a flat on the other side of town as she'd run away from T's brother. She was subject to the same things as I was and was also sick of beatings and street life. But the heroin had already got her. (To this day, she's barely alive. So sad, as she was stunning.) We 'chased the dragon' that day – that's what it's called when you burn it on foil. I remember the smell was horrid. I always think of the film, *Train Spotting* now, when the character sank into the floor. That's how it felt: the most unnatural sensation you could ever have. It made me feel numb and emotionless.

I left her, spaced out, and got on the bus. It went on into town and back twice while I was asleep, face down in my own vomit. I don't even know what I was dreaming of. I was away with the fairies: it's called 'gowching'. When I finally woke up and got off at my stop, I was itching all over and feeling cold. This happened for days. The comedown was horrific. Cold turkey they call it and that's how your skin feels – all prickly and raw.

I thought I was going to die.

What I would tell my younger self about this...

Lessons learnt:

I know now that the drugs were just a way for me to escape; escape the awful reality that had become my life. I was still a child, though, and all of this was foreign to me. I was introduced to a world I hadn't known existed at a vulnerable age. My mother is a devout Catholic. In a way, I guess this was me rebelling against any beliefs that had been embedded into my brain.

S started seeing a guy who was younger than she was. Imagine – I had to keep that a secret from T and his brother. I met her one day but I told T that I was meeting an old friend called Shelly, who I used to dance with. Then, afterwards, just my luck: T bumped into Shelly in town and asked her if we'd had fun on our catch-up. (What were the odds of that?) 'I haven't seen Lyndsey in years,' Shelly replied.

I was visiting a friend on the eighth floor of a tower block of flats. In came T and asked me how my catch-up with Shelly had gone. And I just knew he knew. He picked me up like a ragdoll and threw me down the stairs. He then ran down, dragged me up again by my hair and threw me down again. He did this a few times. It was like torture. As we got to the top, he would punch me in my face and kick me all over. My friend was screaming. There was such fear in her face. The fear I felt. There was blood everywhere – from my nose, my mouth. I couldn't open my eyes or even walk.

T then dragged me out of the flat, punching me in the head; kicking and punching me so hard. I remember thinking, 'Is he going to throw me over the balcony? This is it; I'm going to die.' He was shouting at me that I must have been with a man, and all the time I was protecting S.

He dragged me into the commercial bin area: big, tall, 10-foot round metal bins. Holding me by my chin and hair, he smashed my face against one of them. My head was spinning. Two guys came out of the pub, which was in full view of where this was all happening. They saved my life, I'm sure. They shouted, 'Take your hands off of her!' And he dropped me and ran.

I had a broken nose and more. And I was sure my ears were black and blue, bruised from him grabbing them and shouting in my face. My neck had bruising too. My whole body was black and blue. I looked like the elephant man.

I went to my friend's house as I had nowhere else to go. It had started snowing heavily. I knocked on her door and her mum answered. I really didn't know what else to do. Her mum just looked at me in shock, her hand over her mouth. She said, 'Lyndsey, is that you?!' The panic in her mother's voice led my friend to come running down the stairs. Her face was horrified. I could just make it out, even though I could hardly see out of my eyes. And I collapsed. I was beaten, drained, broken.

I stayed there for a few days and, yes, as T always did, he found me. He came crying, and I mean full on crying. I now know they were just crocodile tears. We went for a walk and he begged me to forgive him. And I did. What a fool I was. As a child I would dream of monsters; I knew they were bad. Yet here I was in love with one.

What I would tell my younger self about this...

Lessons learnt:

The abuse from my father was repeated in my relationship with T, although to a greater extent. In my mind at the time, all I could think was, 'How can I love you so much, and you do this to me?' I didn't know any better. This man was supposed to be the man to save me. He couldn't even save himself.

Chapter Eleven

#Metoo

Attempted rape

One night after midnight, when I was back out on the late-night shift as I called it, I got into a Jaguar car. A dark-haired chap in his thirties was driving. I'm sure he was around that age. He drove me to a car park that was quiet and out of the way from the main roads. He was talking strangely, saying he'd been in prison with a guy from Coventry who had murdered his girlfriend. It was crazy because the night the guy did this to his girlfriend, I was around him in a crack den, smoking with him.

The next minute, the man punched me fully in my face and my nose was bleeding. I said, 'Please, let's go somewhere safer.' There was that fear again inside me, but I had to stay calm; calm for myself if I was going to get out of this situation.

He shouted, 'Don't fuck with me, bitch!' As he drove out of the car park, I pressed a button on the door and the window came down. I crawled out through the opening while he was driving. He grabbed my ankle but I kicked until I was free and I went rolling down the road. Luckily for me, there were a few cars driving past. He shouted, 'I'll be coming for you!' I ran and ran until I got home. My heart was pumping out of my chest, with panic, with fear. I'll never forget the look of evil in his eyes. Later that week, one of the other girls on the beat got taken by him to the woods, and he brutally raped and beat her.

We had a good community on the beat. Us girls, we would always chat and joke with each other. In Coventry then, girls were going missing. Two of the girls I knew have never been found to this day: Roxy and Barbara Finn. The day I had my first daughter is the day Barbara went missing. I'd seen her earlier that same day. I'll never forget her. She was so friendly and caring. She was older than me and she had such a big, caring heart.

Roxy had a few children. She was always singing and dancing on the street corner, telling us all jokes. Those women were a part of my life and I really hope that one day there will be justice for their family and they can be laid to rest.

Rape

He was a middle-aged Scottish man. I can remember his face and his smell as clear as day.

I was on my usual corner on the beat. I got into his car and he took me to his cottage. It was just pushed back off the main road and has actually been knocked down now. I drive past there sometimes and remember that night.

We went into the house and straight upstairs. I felt a little on edge but thought, 'Just go with it, Lyndsey.' The smell of whiskey was so strong on his breath as he got close to me. That's when he started to get more arrogant. I said, 'Let me get a condom out my pocket,' but he began to use force to push me down onto the bed. He then raped me.

I closed my eyes and froze. He was licking my neck, breathing hard in my face. It was over quickly, but it felt like a lifetime.

When he got off me, he didn't say a word as he went to the bathroom. I got up and ran fast out of the house, and I never stopped running until I got home. T wasn't in. In fact he never came home that night. He was out with another woman. That was something else – I was always fighting with other girls over him.

The next morning, I was in the launderette doing our washing, trying to keep my mind off what had happened the night before. In walked T. I told him what had happened and he said to me to get home. I was thinking, 'What have I done?' And as we got into the flat, he beat me up. He said I was lying, and I just wanted sex with the man for free. He beat me more as I hadn't made his £100 again. I was being drilled into the ground.

Fast forward around six months and I was in court on another charge of street-theft. As I was waiting, I saw the guy who had raped me. He was just standing there with a woman. My heart beat out of my chest and I thought, 'What shall I do?'

In that moment, I went over to the security and told them. They called a duty police officer over and the punter was arrested there and then. The woman asked what was going on, so I shouted, 'He raped me!' The look on her face... She was horrified as they took him off. I was told to wait. The days went by and I then had a call: they'd released him due to lack of evidence, so that was the end of that.

What I would tell my younger self about this...

Lessons learnt:

I was still right to speak out. Rape is never ok. Did you know that reported rape offences have risen by around 65%, even though the number of convictions has fallen by 26%. Speak up; speak your truth.

Going nowhere

Give yourself time and you will fly again.

- Karen K Sandhu

Chapter Twelve

Street life

I used to do this with two girls who also worked on the beat: we would take punters back to the flat, keep them in there and steal their bank cards. We would make out that our boyfriends were going to hurt them. One of us would go before midnight and then again after to steal cash from their accounts from the cash point. One time, I stole money from of a Chinese man, and he came back for me. I'm sure he was from a Triad. There were a good few chasing me. How I managed to get away I'll never know. They chased me onto the balcony of the second-floor flat. I had to hop from one balcony to another – flat to flat – and then I just jumped. I was so surprised I didn't break my legs. I went rolling over and over and when I got up, I ran as fast as I could, my heart once again pounding out of my chest; something I was just used to living with now.

Drugs and raving

1990: the days for me of raves, ecstasy, acid tabs. That

feeling it all gave me, like I was the best dancer ever and I loved everyone. I would go to all the raves, dancing until the morning, high out of my face, taking acid tabs and tripping. I had this thing about looking at rice when I got home, and it would be like looking at maggots. Love doves, Bart Simpsons – I would take anything just to get high and numb the pain of my life and how I felt.

Washing crack cocaine (mixing cocaine with bicarbonate of soda which then crystallises into crack) in the flat where I lived with T, we would have crack parties. We would call our friends, who all wanted the crack pipe. You'd see them twitching, craving, waiting for their turn. Then, when they got hold of it, they'd be greedy, wanting to keep it. I'd watch them pick at the carpet; pick at it till the pile came off it, thinking they'd dropped some crack. They were so careful, there was no way they would have done, but that's what crack does to you. It makes you think things and see things that aren't really there. I always seemed to hear noises and people talking 20 times louder than they actually were. It gets you so high, so paranoid.

Chapter Thirteen

Motherhood

I was the thinnest I'd ever been and I was being sick. I didn't get it. Then I thought, 'Am I pregnant?!' I did a test and yep: positive. I was pregnant.

All sorts went through my mind. I was still under the power of T. I'd smoked crack a few times whilst I was pregnant and I currently lived at T's brother's with his girlfriend. It was just a crack house and I needed to get away but it was so hard for me to stop smoking it myself because my mind wanted it. I had a choice: stay and have a crack baby and still be addicted to it, or leave for myself and my unborn child.

That choice turned my life around. My child had to come first.

I left there, stopped smoking crack and went to live with a friend of T's mother. I knew I had to break free; free from the control. And it was soon after that that I went into a hostel.

The hostel

The hostel was an old wartime block. I had a small room with a single bed and a wardrobe. The showers were communal for women, like in the old PE blocks at school. It was cold and creepy, and there were other girls there the same as me – young and pregnant. I was 17 years old.

We did have laughs. We'd tell each other ghost stories and make banging noises on the walls. Some would be there for a few nights; others, like myself, for months on end. But we all did have each other, I guess.

We were given vouchers to eat in the canteen. That's where you'd mix with males, young and older women, drug users, alcoholics; all kinds of lost people. I'll never forget one day being in the meal queue and I had the last shepherd's pie. The lady served me and said to carry on. The next minute, a man shouted, 'The last pie!' And he hit my tray in the air. I was so scared. I was seven months pregnant, alone, with just myself and my unborn child. I panicked and ran back to my cold room, where I sobbed, and I clearly remember asking God, 'Please let us be safe.'

A few days later, through the doom and gloom, a letter arrived for me. My prayers had been answered: the council were offering me a two-bedroom flat. Only it wasn't in a great area – and how freaky that it was actually the flat next door to where I'd been when T had thrown me down the stairs all those times and beaten me for keeping S's secret.

My girlfriends came to see it and said, 'Lyndsey, you don't want your child growing up around here – it's the beat!' And hell, no, that hit home.

The council had given me a £600 grant, which was to buy furniture. But I knew I couldn't live in that area, so I found a private house advertised in the local paper and that was it. I gave the keys back to the council and I went to view the place. I'll never forget my first sight of it. It had black cord carpet throughout, a yellow sofa, a single bed and a wardrobe. I cried as I now had nothing – I'd spent all my £600 on rent for this house for me and my unborn child. But I was going to make it work for us. Something inside me said, 'You can do this, Lyndsey.'

Labour

Having my first daughter made me feel whole as a person. Four hours and she was here, and guess who was with me? Random, but it was S, T's brother's girlfriend. She'd ended up moving into a bedsit next to my house. She was high on crack, but I didn't have anyone else to turn to at the time. So, after the birth, I gave her my key and asked her to bring me some toiletries and clothes. And then I heard nothing more from her. She went to my house, stole my social security money and never came back.

I was in hospital for days with no clean underwear. I felt awful and dirty. And then I had a visitor: T's mother. What a powerful woman. Bless her heart, she took my washing and brought me what I needed – new underwear and nightwear. She was a strict lady with a heart of gold and I'll never forget her. Sadly, she passed away in 2009.

I allowed T around us again. Silly I know, but this guy still had a massive amount of control over me. It was like he was my drug and I really was trapped.

A few months after having my first daughter, I got pregnant again. How was I going to cope? The violence was still happening. So I made the choice: I had an abortion, and when I got home, T beat me because I'd killed his child.

Within a year, I got caught with my second daughter. I was smoking a lot of cigarettes and drinking heavily. I wanted a break. A change. Same as always, T was beating me and stealing from me, even when I was pregnant. One morning, he got up and needed money. I'd paid a deposit on a new sofa. He dragged me by my hair – me being heavily pregnant – the whole way to the shop. My knees were all bruised and bleeding and I had clumps of hair coming out. I remember a lady shouting, 'Get off her!'

T took my deposit off me and smoked it up, so I had to stay with the old yellow sofa that had come with the house.

At the time, I was taking my driving lessons. One day, at 33 weeks pregnant, I was having a lesson when I began to get pains. I said to my instructor, 'I'm having my baby. I just know it...' His face was a picture. We grabbed my friend from her house, and literally as we got to the hospital and I lay on the bed for an examination – whoosh! My waters broke and went everywhere. The midwife just caught my daughter in her hands. She was 3lb 3oz: my blessing.

One of the hardest things I had to cope with was that they put me on a ward with women who had given birth to their babies, and they had their babies with them. But my daughter was down in special care. I cried myself to sleep that night just wanting to be with her.

She spent six weeks in special care. My older daughter and I would visit every day. We had to take two buses to get there and we missed her so much. But she was growing.

I'll never forget one day when we went to visit. The ward had three rooms. As the babies progressed, they moved up. We arrived to find my baby wasn't in the first room. In panic, I screamed, 'Where's my baby?' The nurse looked confused and I thought she must have passed away. I broke down.

Then a doctor said, 'Don't panic, she's here. She's getting better. Her lungs are expanding and she's moved up a room.' I'd never felt so relieved.

But not long after, T arrived, shouting at me that I hadn't told him our baby had been moved, as if I'd known about it and had kept it from him. The doctors looked on in shock but T didn't care. He had no thought for me or our child.

She grew stronger and my older daughter and I continued travelling to see her daily. Then, six weeks later, we took her home.

Home. We always wanted it to be a happy place. But it was never that.

The beatings

Most days were the same. I would be on edge wondering whose house T was going to be in – mine or the other woman's. I'd get up some mornings to find my TV had been sold or once even my car. He'd sold them for crack and I'd have to buy them back. I remember the time I didn't do something he wanted quick enough. He got a metal coat hanger, unravelled it and whipped me with it. Then he urinated over me. The pain, the stinging, was horrendous. I remember thinking, 'Please, God, let this stop.' He fractured my arm and broke my nose a few more times. Once he came in and I was half asleep. All I remember after that was waking up, choking on my tongue. He'd knocked me unconscious and he was crying, trying to get my tongue out. I forever had black eyes; bruises all over me; cuts and lumps in my head. I could go on and on. I was always dropping the charges on him; the fear was terrible. I had no self-worth and my children saw far too much. And I was still only a child myself – 20 years of age by now.

I remember us going to Barbados with his mother, and he even beat me up there. The kids were screaming. This was all because an artist called Red Rat had sung to me. Whenever we went away he'd beat me up.

One day I was at work and I didn't feel at all well. When I got home, T was there telling me to get him an ambulance as he was ill. When the ambulance arrived, the paramedics were more concerned about me. I could barely breathe. I got them to call a friend to come and stay with my girls while T came with me to the hospital. His face looked so angry and I'll never forget how he kicked the wheelchair I was sitting in, saying, '*I'm* the one who's sick!'

The pain in my chest was horrendous. It felt worse than labour pains and I didn't even want to breathe. I was in hospital for two weeks. I had blood tests, scans, x-rays. The weight just fell off me. I sat on the bed one day, crying for help. I called to the nurse, not wanting to speak. She sat with me and showed me how to bring up the phlegm from my chest. I gagged as I did it and cried with pain.

My friend came and bathed me as I had no energy. I had drips in both arms and I was so frail, losing more weight, and I was tiny anyway. I eventually went down to 4.5 stone. After a few days, my results came back: I had pneumonia and I really thought I was going to die from it. T came up once and brought my girls. Gosh, how I missed them! He never bothered to ask how I was. He just sat there. You could see the jealous look in his eyes; jealous that the nurses were caring for me.

What I would tell my younger self about this...

Lessons learnt:

I realise looking back now that T was quite the narcissist. He always had to be the centre of attention. Even when I was at my weakest, this man couldn't put his ego aside to realise I was in great pain. I am glad that I called the ambulance, though. I saved myself.

Chapter Fourteen

Wedding bells

The move

The house we lived in wasn't in a nice area. There were holes in the ceilings and the floors.

I got a move from a housing association, but the rule was I wasn't allowed to let T near us as they were aware of the violence through the courts. However, T being T, I was bullied. We moved into the new house. It was lovely for me and the girls, but again I was drawn under his control. He asked me to marry him and I said yes. All I ever wanted for my girls was a family and I thought this was the right thing to do. This was the norm for society.

The wedding

Everyone was shocked. Not one member of my family wanted me to marry him. I remember my mother saying, 'Lyndsey, don't.' I was 25. Ten years had passed since T and

I had first got together and I was making a choice that I thought was the right one at the time.

I borrowed my wedding dress from a lady I worked with and I paid for the whole wedding myself. T never paid a penny. Through the weeks building up to the day itself, there was just so much tension.

When the morning arrived, my friend did my hair and make-up and then I put on the dress. That's when I thought to myself, 'Lyndsey, are you really doing the right thing for you and your children?' But I'd made a choice: this was it, make or break. Arriving at the church, there were so many people. I felt sick inside; T actually made me feel sick. What was I doing? When the vicar said, 'Does anyone object to this wedding?' T looked around and thought it was funny. I was looking to see if any other women he was seeing had turned up. There were so many people there, just to see if we really were going to get married. Hundreds of them. The reception afterwards was amazing, with everyone dancing, enjoying the day into the night. I remember thinking, 'How are all these people even here? And who are a lot of them anyway?'

As the day came to an end, my older daughter didn't want to leave me. And I really didn't want to leave my girls but they were taken home by my mother. T and I then went off to a hotel. I thought, 'Please don't even touch me.'

Then it hit me: 'Lyndsey, you have literally made it to break it.' He repulsed me.

A few days after we were married, the beatings began again. One evening, T came home and started on me again for no reason as he never needed one. He hit my head on the staircase and split it open. My girls were in bed. I was trying to keep the situation calm. I remember thinking, 'No way is this ever happening to me again.'

I said I needed ice as my head was pouring with blood. My mind was in overdrive. I had to get out of the house but how was I going to? I said, 'Let's go get some ice,' trying to keep him calm, as his nostrils were flaring up at me and he was pushing his face into mine as he always had done for years. But now, somehow I felt different. I felt calmer inside.

'The shop on the corner's still open,' I said.

'Don't you try and be clever and run off,' he answered, and proceeded to kick me out of the house and all along the street.

As we turned the corner to the shop, as if my guardian angels were watching over me, there – right there – was a police car. T had me in a head lock and I screamed for help so loud that the police rushed over. I didn't feel scared then. I had this strength come over me and I pushed him away and shouted at the police to arrest him.

T was arrested there and then. As the police threw him to the ground, he was screaming, 'Get off me!' and, 'Lyndsey, please don't do this to me!' All those years, that was me doing the begging and now it was him. His power over me from that day was taken away. I felt like the weight of the last ten years had been lifted. He was sent to prison straightaway. The prosecution were over the moon and said, 'Lyndsey, this should have happened years ago!'

The amount of times T had bullied me into dropping the charges was unreal. The photo evidence of my wounds for years was awful. And in that moment, I broke free from him forever.

He received three months in prison, with an order to stay away with the power of arrest. I told myself, 'Lyndsey, you're not living in fear of this man anymore.' I think now that this was the real turning point for me. I knew I was changing; growing up and putting my and my children's safety first.

Growing as a person

I started going out more and enjoying life again. I enrolled on a college course in counselling and found myself on a work placement in a drug rehab. The rehab was run by Christians and the residents worked on a 12-week programme focusing on maintenance, cooking and gardening. It was males only, mostly from the north of the UK.

One day, a fight broke out in the kitchen and one of the residents went to stab another. I calmly said, 'Stop,' and I won the man over there and then. I felt calm inside. I'd been in situations like this many times myself. T's brother once held a knife to my throat and to his. I just knew how to stay calm. It's crazy really how, just in that moment, something kicks in and you manage to keep your cool. So life was feeling better. I was working again, putting on weight and feeling more confident in myself. I felt I had a new purpose.

What I would tell my younger self about this...

Lessons learnt:

This was the first realisation I had of my love for helping others. I loved the environment we created in the rehabilitation centre. I loved helping these people get their lives back on track.

On the right track?

Without the rain, there would be no rainbow.

- Karen K Sandhu

Chapter Fifteen

New relationship

I met my son's father in a club. He was very handsome and funny. He'd not long got out of prison for getting into a fight, and had done 15 years for murder. (I know what you're thinking: was I nuts?) But I'm a believer in people making mistakes and being given a second chance. He and his brother had got into a fight with a gang in a pub in London. At the time, there was a knife amnesty on. The judge sentenced them both to life in prison. However, he'd been released at Her Majesty's pleasure.

We dated for two years before we made the commitment to move in together. I'd bought my house by this time and it was my dream home. The house I'd drawn in the car park when I was seven had manifested into my reality. I was finally living in it: the law of attraction really was working for me.

When I caught pregnant with my son, this pregnancy was different. There was no stress. We were all so happy for the next four years. I'd finally got my family. I had rhinoplasty surgery on my nose – as you know, it had been broken so many times. I also treated myself to a boob job! We went on some amazing holidays too; shared some really great, fun times; opened up a tanning shop together; and took money out of the house, which was in my name, to buy a flat in his name as an investment. B was my best friend. The connection and the friendship we had was amazing and so powerful.

Then the cracks started to show.

My son was three years old and he wasn't great at sleeping through the night. And most of the night, B would be out. Then money started to go missing. He was moody. I could see all the signs but I was trying to block them out, telling myself, not again, not crack cocaine. B went from being funny and loving, to arrogant and on edge. He was like a ticking time bomb waiting to go off. As the year went on, I lost my best friend and my children lost their father and father figure. I couldn't believe what was happening. I tried to reach out to him so many times but the lies continued. And the money continued to go missing; thousands of pounds gone.

He would disappear for days. I'd call him at 2am and if he did answer, he'd say he was fixing the roof over at our sunbed shop. He'd bribe my daughters to lie for him too. They were none the wiser. He'd let them stay out late at night, have all of their friends over, and he'd even buy them alcohol. Of course, to my teenage daughters, this was absolute heaven. Their stepfather was the coolest. They didn't notice what I'd been noticing for a long time. I didn't come to learn about the bribery for quite a while.

I remember, just before my 35th birthday, I received a phone call from him saying that he'd been abducted and I had to buy him back. I'd tried so hard to make it work but the drugs had taken over by this time and there was no hope.

One night he returned home but didn't enter the house. He sat in his car on the driveway, staring up at the windows, demented. My daughters and I watched him from a bedroom at the front of the house. My younger daughter began sleeping with a kitchen knife in her bedside drawer after this; something else I didn't come to know until years later.

There was one night when I confronted him about it. My daughters were staying at friends' houses, and it was just me, him and my son at home. He locked the outside doors to the house and began to attack me. We had a small bathroom at the front downstairs, with a tiny little window. I managed to climb through this and run out of the house towards an old friend's place, who lived around the corner. It was where my younger daughter was staying. As I was running, I noticed he'd begun to chase me in his car. The first realisation was that he'd left our son in bed by himself. I was mortified. I reached my friend's house to get help as I needed to get my son out. My daughter, who was only 14 at the time, immediately ran to our house with her friend. B tried to fight her for my son as she lifted him out of his bed. Luckily, there was a bottle of aftershave on the counter and, quick-thinking as she is, she sprayed it in his eyes and ran for her life.

I had to think of my and my children's future. He was still going to work as a forklift truck driver. I don't know how he did it. He was a functional user. But I made the choice to leave. I called him one day when he was at work and told him not to come back. He had restrictions on him as he was on licence for life, so he had to stay away. He then moved into the flat that we'd bought, but after a few months, it got taken from him by the mortgage company.

I took my children on holiday as a way to take their minds off the horrible atmosphere at home, and I allowed them to each bring a friend. Whilst we were away, I received phone calls to tell me that B had vandalised our sunbed shop. Then, when we returned, we found he'd broken into our home and stolen from us. He'd not only taken from me, he'd stolen gifts he'd bought for my children too. That was the final nail in the coffin. I wanted nothing more to do with him.

What I would tell my younger self about this...

Lessons learnt:

I wish I'd listened to my intuition earlier and, once the first signs of drug use appeared, that I'd confronted him then. It was hard for me to accept that my fairy-tale romance had come to an end. Drugs change people, and to watch it happen before your own eyes is utterly heart-breaking.

Chapter Sixteen

Changes

Being on my own with my children again felt strange. There was a sense of mourning. I felt my whole world had been broken. I had to give myself that push to keep moving forward. 'Come on, Lyndsey,' I told myself, 'look where you've been!' I knew it was time to put my focus into where I wanted to go.

My son had now started school and I enrolled on a gym course at a local college. It was amazing to connect with new people. I got myself a job in the gym, which meant that the college paid for my personal training course. Everything was starting to go well again and I was feeling better within myself. The first time I sat my level 3 fitness exam, I failed. It was a tough time for me as I'd revised so hard, to the point that it was all I'd talk about to anyone who'd listen! However, I picked myself back up, resat the examination, and this time I passed.

Fitness for me was a whole new world. I was connecting with some great people. I then started my Les Mills journey, which is group exercise and coaching in front of large groups of people. This was great for boosting my confidence. Helping people in group classes really helped me too for sure. As well as this, my children were shining again and doing well at school. They had a few arguments as kids do, but we'd go on some amazing holidays with some wonderful friends.

For my older daughter's prom, my younger daughter contacted an agent through a site and arranged for DJ Ironik, a music artist my older daughter loved, to chaperone her to her prom and perform for all the school prom year. We got on so well that we stayed in touch and are in contact even now. His agent, who is actually his mother, has become my good friend – my 'Char'. She's such a lovely soul, and we're so alike she's like my soul sister.

Ironik would invite me to his birthday parties. They were incredible and celebs from the music industry would be there. I was living such a different life from my time among the crack dens. Who would have thought I'd be mixing with people like this, and not trash anymore?

Ironik's uncle, Steve Gordon, is the founder of Twice As Nice Music. We got on so well together that he'd invite me to his events, from London to Skegness to Ibiza. It was just a breath of fresh air. I'd be backstage with various music artists, literally living the dream, and we were like one big family – as Steve called it, the Twice As Nice family.

Coming face to face with my dad

Around this time, my dad was giving my mum a hard time. He was turning up drunk at her house, where she lived with my stepdad, in the early hours of the morning.

I don't know what happens, but sometimes you just find the strength in the moment. I was driving home one day and I suddenly turned left into the road where he lived. His house was only about ten minutes from mine. I pulled up outside and knocked on the door. His wife answered. Her face was in shock when she saw me.

'Lyndsey,' she said, 'is that you?'

'Yes,' I said. 'Is my dad in?'

She shouted to him and told me to go through. She seemed very withdrawn, like her mind was all over the place. I went through to the kitchen. He was sitting in a chair with his head down. I knew he couldn't walk very well as he now had arthritis.

I said to him, 'Look up at me.' In that moment, I felt a powerful energy and I wasn't scared. I said, 'Never go near my mum again. You're no father of mine. Not after the way you treated me as a child.'

His head hung even lower. And all I could see was this weather-beaten old man.

That was the last any of us ever heard from him. I'd faced my fear of my dad and, as I took a deep breath and left his house, that was that. I don't know why that was the right time but it was. Now I was free from him forever.

What I would tell my younger self about this...

Lessons learnt:

It wasn't his fault how he was brought up, so forgive and close the chapter. I've let it go now and moved on.

Chapter Seventeen

The big 'C' word

It was 2011. I was 36 years old and having irregular bleeding. I was just having some fun with a guy at the time (yes, sexual fun) when this would happen: I would bleed. Bleed a lot. There was no pain just a lot of blood.

I went to the doctor and he said it was inflammation of the cervix. He gave me a course of antibiotics and sent me on my way. It then happened again a few weeks later. There was a cover doctor on when I went back. She was very caring and she took her time with me. It was March and I wasn't due a smear test until July, but she gave me a test, just to be on the safe side. I'm so grateful that she did. A few weeks went by before my results came back. They showed unusual cells. Within several days, I was in having a large part of my cervix removed. The nurses explained to me that it would be sent off for testing and I'd hear from them.

That weekend, I went to Marbella with a friend, partying away as I love to do. Then, on the Sunday afternoon, I was chilling in Ocean Club when my phone rang. A lady's voice said, 'Hi, Lyndsey, can you talk?' It was the nurse from the hospital. She said I needed to go in straightaway. My head was suddenly all over the place. What was happening? I was so confused. I asked her if it was to do with the results and she said, yes, but she didn't want to go into it over the phone.

I took a deep breath and got a flight home first thing on the Monday morning, not knowing what I was about to hear. I met up with a friend, who really supported me and kept me calm through this time, and we went to the hospital together. As we walked in, there were three Macmillan nurses waiting for me. One was the nurse I'd seen before, who was also the nurse who had given me the news on the phone. I was very nervous but my friend was calm. I'm so glad I had her there. She's a nurse herself so was used to these types of conversations.

In came the doctor. I remember him coming straight to the point: 'You have grade 3 cervical cancer, Lyndsey.'

I didn't understand. I thought that when they cut away my cervix, it would have gone. I said, 'Am I going to die?' I'll never forget the way the three nurses just looked at me with blank expressions. No one was saying anything.

The doctor said, 'We'll need you to have an MRI scan to check if the cancer has travelled through your lymph node.' If it had, I was told I'd need chemo and radiotherapy. I froze but knew I had to be strong. It was fight or flight and I had to fight this.

I was booked in for the following week. My friend and I left the hospital and went to my mum's house to tell her.

She was very calm, which was what I needed. Her words were, 'You will fight this, Lyndsey, I know you will.'

And she was right. On the way to see her, I'd really thought, 'Right, Lyndsey, you have this and you'll deal with it with positive energy. You're strong and you can fight it. Don't let it get you.' A few days later, I had the MRI scan. It was a really strange experience. I wasn't allowed to move and I'm a person who can't sit still. After I'd had the scan, the doctor said, 'It's now just a question of waiting on the results.' So I had to play the waiting game and stay positive.

Through this time, I was taking time out for myself, eating well and resting, and a random message came up on my Twitter account so I replied. The guy seemed really nice – he was a football player – and we had some good chats. We ended up speaking every day for a few weeks. Then he said he was coming to the UK and invited me down to London to have a night out in a top venue. As I was waiting on my results, I turned the invitation down. His response was, 'Don't you know who I am?!' I just thought, 'Not my kind of person really,' but then I hadn't told him my story and about what was happening in my life at the time.

When I next took a walk to my local shop, just to clear my head, that same man was on the front of a newspaper on the counter. I asked the shop assistant, 'Who's that?' The assistant told me and said he was a multi-million-pound player! I was in shock but I just had to let it go. And I think now it wasn't meant to be.

That weekend, I went back to Marbella, partied and had so much fun with friends. I had in my mind all the time that this cancer wasn't going to beat me. Again, whilst in Ocean Club, my phone rang and it was the hospital. I took a deep breath... My results were back. The cancer hadn't spread. I felt such a relief knowing this! There and then, I was booked in for a full hysterectomy the same week.

The operation

The day arrived. I kept very positive. I wasn't going to lose my good mindset. My mum came with me and we were joking about things in life whilst I was waiting; just making the time pass. I was given a gown, socks and a hair net, and we joked about how I looked.

I was very uncertain about how I'd feel after the operation. I'd had surgery before but nothing like this. 'Lyndsey Austin,' someone called out, 'time to go.' I said to my mum, 'See you on the other side,' and I smiled and waved to her, singing the song, 'So Long, Farewell' as they pushed me away in the wheelchair. I was just trying to make her laugh. She did say to me, 'You are funny, Lyndsey.'

Seven hours later, I woke up and, gosh, I felt like I'd been hit by a bus. The pain was horrendous. My feet were together but my knees had dropped apart. My mum had gone to look after my children and a friend was there. I remember saying, 'You look so pretty and I feel shit,' as I zoned in and out on morphine.

The doctor came to check up on me and said I'd need seven days in hospital to recover. But me being me, I was out in three days. I pushed myself; I was a fitness coach, I had this. I had all the ladies on the ward laughing too, as I told my funny stories. We had this deal that when you did a number two, you had to do the Michael Jackson moon dance across the ward! That would mean it was closer to when you could go home because your body was recovering well.

A student nurse came to see me to tell me about my surgery. She said they basically hung me nearly upside down, packed my organs and removed my womb and my glands. They kept my ovaries hitched up either side of my waist during the procedure. No wonder I felt so terrible afterwards! But I stayed positive and pushed forward within those first three days. One of my close friends always says I brushed it off. It was just me believing: I can get through this.

My message to you:

Ladies, any sign of irregular bleeding, please get it checked. Look after you and be strong.

Scar

The scar from my operation is seven inches across. I got very body-conscious afterwards. I'd put on a little weight as I wasn't exercising and my flat stomach was no more. I rang the surgeon who'd done my rhinoplasty to ask for a tummy tuck. His answer was no, of course.

I also had a problem that when I walked, sometimes my leg would collapse on my left side because the operation had hit a nerve. I had acupuncture to try to help with this. I'd have pins put in my back, and my leg would shoot upwards. It was so bizarre. This went on for at least four months. I needed to give my body a chance to heal and I had to accept that.

What I would tell my younger self about this...

Lessons learnt:

My body was never going to look the same again and I had to allow myself time to heal properly. But I still had my life – and that's far more important.

Chapter Eighteen

Ibiza, baby!

One thing I'll say about Steve Gordon is that he treated us all so well. We were part of a great team of friends.

It was September 2011 and I was at the Twice As Nice closing parties in Ibiza. And what a blast it was. Though I'd been many times before, this was different. I'd put on weight and was still recovering from my operation. The thought of putting a bikini on scared me, but I braved it. Me, Char and the girls were off. We stayed at the same hotel as DJ Ironik, Artful Dodger, Creed and CKP, and the fun and laughs we had that holiday were brilliant. Life memories. It's so great to know such amazing people.

CKP and I had a deep conversation one day walking to the beach. He'd lost his mother a few years before and we were talking about life and how grateful we should be to live the life we do. I told him how I felt about my scar and how my body had changed. I'll never forget his words: 'Be true to yourself and love the skin you're in.' And those words are so right.

I tell myself now: 'This is your scar, Lyndsey. Love yourself. Love who you are. Always be body-confident. Embrace it and be glad to be alive.'

And, ladies, I would say the same to you: love your scars and your stretch marks. They are you and your story.

I didn't go back to work for six months. My body certainly needed the time to recover and I had to have regular check-ups. I'm now nine years in remission and very grateful. Getting back into teaching my classes was a push for my body. Big changes had happened to it. I had an empty feeling on the inside but I gave myself the time I needed.

What I would tell my younger self about this...

Lessons learnt:

I realised I had to slow down. I was always rushing around and now I know to take things more slowly.

Chapter Nineteen

The big 40!

My fortieth birthday was amazing. As I've said, I've had so many great holidays, but I took my daughters and some friends with me for this one. There were 11 of us in total and what an amazing time we had. We touched down in Marbella and we had it all planned: the pool parties, the nightclubs, and we had our own beds and tables booked. The drinks flowed, the music was fantastic and we all had the time of our lives. To this day, the girls say it was one of the best holidays they've ever had. We call it the 'hangover holiday', just like the film.

My message to you:

We all go through tough times in life but you can still make special memories that will stay with you forever.

Barbados: April 2014

Now, being the big 40, my son and I and a friend went to Barbados. Our ground-floor apartment was right on the beach front in Crystal Waters, with golden sands and there was a small beach bar next to it.

We got talking to some locals and my son was break-dancing and having fun, when a few of the local guys joined in. One of them did a backflip and a gun dropped out of the back pocket of his trousers. My son and my friend froze but I was calm. It wasn't like it was anything I hadn't seen before. The man said, 'It's ok, I'm a policeman – drug squad.' At which point, everyone calmed down and laughed.

We all had a few drinks together and the man gave me his number and said to hook up with him and he'd show us around the island. The next day, I told my friend I'd phone him and take him up on his offer. When he answered, he said hello in such a lovely tone. We chatted but I couldn't really understand his Bajan dialect very well, so we joked about that.

He said he'd come and see us soon and when he turned up, my friend shouted, 'Your friend's here!' – and there he was. My heart flipped. He had on a white vest, denim jeans and shades. It was like watching a guy out of Miami Vice strolling up the beach! He was so hot! Was I tipsy the night before, or something, that I hadn't noticed this? It's crazy what we notice sometimes more than others.

He took us all on a little tour that early evening. Around The Gap were bars where soka music was playing. Later, my friend offered to have my son, and A and I went back to our local bar. The fun we had was out of this world. I felt so free and happy. I said to him, 'Let's do the dance from *Dirty Dancing,* ('Time of my Life'). So he went to the other end of the bar and I was at the top. We danced, I made the jump and he caught me – and in that moment, I felt alive and so happy. People were smiling, laughing, clapping us – it was amazing just being in that moment of joy.

For the rest of the holiday, A would go to work then catch up with us afterwards. I really was having the time of my life.

When it was time to go home, the thought of leaving was sad. At the airport, A and I hugged. It was one of those 'when will we see each other again?' moments. But he called me as soon as he'd left me at the airport and said he was coming to the UK to spend time with us. And within a week, he had his flight booked and he was here in less than a month.

We had one disagreement during that time: he and my son were play-fighting and my son caught and broke his watch. A went into a mood for the whole day afterwards – like a child, I thought. They say we should spot the red flags – alert, alert, alert! – and we should pay attention to them. But I thought, 'Give him time. He's away from his home, his family, his children.' He had two young girls – twins. He was missing them was my guess.

As the weeks went by, we spoke about life and being together. 'I want to be with you and your son, Lyns,' he told me.

I talked to my girls about it. They weren't very happy. They both have a fear of me being hurt again, especially my older daughter. By this time, she had a daughter of her own – my beautiful granddaughter, and my youngest daughter was about to have her first.

When we went round to see my second grandchild, I was so excited. A just sat there and didn't speak. Yes, the cracks were showing (red flag alert again), but I was trying to believe it would all be all right.

I applied to the government for him to come and live in the UK. There was a lot of paperwork to do and we'd also have to get married for this to happen. As A went back to Barbados with this dream we both had, I was here doing all the paperwork and getting references from my friends, while A was doing the same with his friends. Then we could send them to the government to prove that we had a relationship and that it could work.

Who was I kidding...?

What I would tell my younger self about this...

Lessons learnt:

I had that feeling in my gut again; that sense of uncertainty – the red flag. And that's the feeling I should have followed.

Chapter Twenty

Wedding bells #2?

By now it was summer and we'd been together for three months. A came back to the UK and everything was officially in place for him to make the move here permanently. There was just one more thing: we needed to get married.

Before he arrived, I'd booked for us to go to Barcelona for our birthdays, as they were only six days apart. When he got here, I was packing our bags to go away when I found a box among his things and inside was an engagement ring. Of course, I wasn't supposed to have seen it and I didn't have a great feeling about it either. But I went along with it, thinking, I just wanted happiness.

We arrived in Barcelona and I felt like a tour guide. I wasn't having the best time and didn't really want to be there (red flag again).

That night, we went out for dinner. There was a strange vibe. Neither of us were sitting comfortably with each other.

Then, all of a sudden, A got down on one knee and asked me to marry him. I said a yes, but inside I was thinking,

'Noooo!' He put the ring on my finger and it felt tight. It didn't fit. The whole thing really was doomed from the start.

Back in the UK, we told my friends and my children the news, and watched the false looks of happiness on their faces. Later, A and I had such a big argument. We just weren't ready for this.

The day came for me to take A back to the airport. The silence on the journey wasn't nice. He gave me a hug and off he went. I really had a sick feeling in my gut.

Then, low and behold, a week later A posted pictures of himself all over social media with another woman. I was so upset. How could he embarrass me so publicly like this? When I say I cried – I really cried. I'd been beaten down by men my whole life, and now this on social media for the world to see. I ended up having to take weeks off work. I lost weight. I felt loss, confusion and shame. Was it my past making me feel like this? That little girl in me just wanting to be loved? I really needed answers.

I spent the next year flying backwards and forwards to Barbados and A would come over here, and we tried to work it out: did we love each other? But we'd just have the same conversations – how would it work? We even went for a meal the following year on Valentine's day; on the beach, still trying to see if we could get our relationship to work. We were just repeating the same thing.

The last time, everything was different. We only caught up for a short while and he was very cold. Was there really anything to talk about now a year had gone by? It was Crop Over Festival in Barbados and that's carnival time. I was there with a friend. I had my feathers on and I danced with thousands of people. Rihanna was on the float in front of ours, singing wild songs. The energy was so powerful.

At the end of the carnival, I couldn't find my friend and I made the choice to call A. I was in a part of Barbados where I didn't know anyone, and I was giving the young children bits of my costume – my jewellery, my headdress. Their little faces looked so happy. It was then that A arrived and took me back to my hotel.

That was when I got my closer. We had that final conversation. And the conversation was silence.

What I would tell my younger self about this...

Lessons learnt:

What I tell myself now is to always take notice of the red flags in any relationship and to understand that a good relationship takes time to build.

Chapter Twenty-one

Suicidal thoughts

In 2015, I hit a low point in my life. Money wasn't coming in as well as I wanted it to and I felt fear: fear of being alone and unloved. All my childhood pain came flooding back. I just wanted to be held and supported. I'd drop my son to school, then sit in my bedroom crying all day, asking God to help me. I wouldn't speak to my friends or daughters about this. I was telling myself, 'I'm not good enough'; thinking of how I could take my own life. Tablets – no, that would be a slow pain. Hanging – yes, that would be quick. At that moment, I didn't give my children a thought.

Then – STOP. 'Lyndsey,' I thought, 'the person who'd find you would be your son and he's 12 years of age.' And that's what stopped me. In that thought, in that moment, I knew I had to find myself. I never wanted that feeling again. Something in my life had to change. I needed to rediscover that lost little girl who just wanted to be loved.

What I would tell my younger self about this...

Lessons learnt:

I'd reached the lowest low and I needed to understand that there really is more to life. I'd beaten a drug addiction and I'd beaten cancer. And I know now that a breakdown is a breakthrough.

The breakthrough

She spread her wings and began to fly.

- Karen K Sandhu

Chapter Twenty-two

Personal and spiritual development

I came across a book by Anthony Robbins called *Unlimited Power*. The impact this book had on me was huge (even though I didn't know what half the words the writer used meant!) and I wanted to learn more about the power of creating the life I wanted to have. *The Universe Has Your Back* by Gabrielle Bernstein was just as empowering: how to be in line with the universe, stepping out of the fear to love, and loving *yourself*. At first I thought, 'Hey, who does that?' I thought loving yourself meant, 'Look at me – aren't I lovely!'

I then came across an event on personal development advertised on Facebook. I booked on and was so excited to see what this would bring for me. When I arrived, there were a good few hundred people already there and all the chairs were set out in rows. I rushed to the front and got a seat right in the middle. A speaker came on, Allan Kleynhans, and music started to play. I wondered what was happening. This wasn't a party, was it? I was a little confused when everyone stood up, dancing a little, and joined in with Allan, who was clapping along. The energy and the vibes in the room were so high.

Then we all took our seats and started to listen. Allan's story was incredibly powerful. I found myself relating to him in so many ways. My eyes were filling up with tears as I listened to his pain, then how he transformed himself. I was there, wanting to put my hand up. I felt I wanted to get on the stage too and tell *my* story!

That was the start of my personal development journey. I knew I needed to grow more as a person in order to heal myself.

After this, I went to every event I could to learn what I needed to about myself. Personal growth became my mission. I wanted to be the best life coach ever.

At one event in Reading, I met a lovely lady. She was so kind and had had a hard time herself in life, so we could relate. She told me about NLP (Neuro-Linguistic Programming) and how it would educate me on how the mind works – the conscious and the unconscious mind, setting goals, anchoring – and also on the big words that Tony and Gabby used in their books. During the breaktime, we sat down, went online and found an online course in NLP. I booked onto it there and then. I was so excited. I really felt I was taking a leap of faith – the kind that gives you that great feeling of butterflies in your belly.

My message to you:

I learnt that taking the action I did was one of the best things I've ever done. So, if you're passionate about something, take that leap and go for it!

The random holiday: 2017

Another great time was so random. A friend asked me to fly out to Europe with her so I said, 'Hell, yes!' If cancer had taught me anything, it was to take every opportunity you can, so I did. And I really did have an amazing time and met some wonderful people.

There was a man there who caught my eye. I mean that literally – you know, when you look into someone's eyes and into their soul. I'd never experienced that before. For the next two years, I'd catch up with him for a bit of fun. There was something there for me: the connection, the conversations. And certain conversations in particular were like mirroring myself. I did become attached to him but I knew I couldn't be with him. He was married, and getting involved with a married man is something I've never been about.

But by this time, I had so much confusion going on in my head. My feelings for this guy were growing. I'd think to myself, 'What if we could be together? How would we be together?' In my mind, he'd come with me everywhere I went: shopping, work, parents' evenings. But I knew deep down it was just me wanting; me being that little girl again and wanting to be loved. I'd say to myself, 'Lyndsey, you're supposed to be on your personal journey of loving *you*, not putting all of you into someone else.' I'd done that all my life. When was I really going to love myself?

What I would tell my younger self about this...

Lessons learnt:

I look back now and realise it was all a dream; a fantasy I'd created in my own mind – ruminating about what we *could have*. The truth is, you may only ever get that connection with someone once in your life. But the only way to really know a person is to spend time around them. And you'll only *truly* know if you've got that connection when you *truly* know the person.

Chapter Twenty-three

Transformation

I finally knew I had to do this for *me*. I managed to track down Allan Kleynhans and we spoke on the phone. He had a course running in London on personal development, so I took that leap again and said, 'Right, book me on.' And it was great. I studied how the mind works, about our thoughts and feelings, and what triggers us to do what we do. I learnt so much about NLP. The course training took me a year to complete and a lot of hours of pushing myself. But I wanted to do it so much and, when I passed, I was over the moon with excitement.

What I learnt was that if you really want something that badly, keep pushing until you get the end result you want. Invest everything you have in yourself.

Allan's course in personal development was so powerful and I met more incredible people. Allan took us through how to tell our story the way we'd do it onstage: talking about our pain points and speaking it all without fear or upset. That took me four days to learn how to do. The first day I was so scared. Although I stand onstage when I teach my fitness classes, this was in no way the same. As soon as I stood up, I felt naked. My truth, all my shame: I was opening up and telling strangers my story. I froze. I could feel the palms of my hands sweating and my legs were shaking. All eyes were on me. I didn't feel comfortable even in the clothes I was wearing. I felt like that scared little girl again (one of the reasons I feel now that what you wear really does have an impact on how you feel inside).

We worked on our stories every day and, by the end of the fourth day, I'd cracked it. There were so many tears, from me and from the others there. Allan also performed inner-child work with us in a meditation and, wow, did I cry. All that has ever happened to me, all that I've written about in this book, came out. Music played low as he took us back to our seven-year-old selves. We had to close our eyes and picture ourselves. I took myself back to my bedroom in the house where I'd lived with my dad. There I was, sitting on the bottom bunk, crying as I always did when I wet the bed. I reached out and gave my seven-year-old self the biggest hug, and I said, 'Lyndsey, we've got this...'

As I opened my eyes, I was sobbing. I really felt like my heart had been cracked open. I then shared what had happened with the group. Every one of them listened without judgement and to me that was powerful, as I felt like I'd been judged all my life. From my past, Allan helped me pull apart all the layers.

They say you are over the pain of your story when you can tell it without tears or fear or shame. And that's me: that's where I am in my life right now.

Getting a coach: January 2019

What I needed was to get a coach. Having someone see in me what I couldn't see in myself had a great impact on my life. My coach taught me a lot about myself. In one session, I broke down, sobbing, bringing the past year up to the surface again. I just couldn't let that man go. But my coach's words were so true: the hardest relationships to get over are the ones that we never really had. That hit home for me, because deep down – and I mean way deep down – who should come first? *You.* It all starts with you. You are your thoughts and what you create. I learnt that there's a big difference between confidence and self-worth. I grew up never really having any personal boundaries, so I had no self-worth. I was a people-pleaser. Now I understand it's ok to say no and to put myself first. I also realise it's time to stop just giving and be more open to receiving. And having a better relationship with money is important too: knowing that everything I need is coming to me, all in good time, and understanding that stressing doesn't change anything.

I learnt to journal: write down how I feel; what I *don't* want and what I *do* want. Also the person I *don't* want to be and the person I *do* want to be, what makes me happy and what makes me sad.

Forgiveness

Through my journey, I've learnt to forgive. That has been healing, instead of unforgiveness eating away at me.

I forgive my dad and my children's fathers for all that has happened. They have a past too and maybe they didn't know how to love. You see, that's the thing: everyone has a journey. I choose to let them go with love and I wish them well.

My message to you:

So, forgive yourself and others who have hurt you. Let go of the emotional and physical pain; all the negative emotion. Forgive them for all they've done. Let it go and make it a choice to heal.

What I would tell my younger self about this...

Lessons learnt:

Working on myself was my healing.

Chapter Twenty-four

Unstoppable

Unstoppable: that's how I felt the moment I connected with an amazing coach from Canada on a social networking site. We had a conversation over Zoom and I told her everything about my life. As I talked, I felt no shame at all. Her jaw dropped. She said I had so much to give to people. Her actual words were: 'Girl, you need to be out there telling your story. Your vibe and your energy are amazing – you need to get out of your own way.'

I felt empowered and I had this fire in my belly, knowing that I needed to be serving people. Another lady I connected with said the same thing. And with work and persistence, I did it. I really did get out of my own way and I took that step. I'd been hiding and the world was waiting for me to show up.

Part 2

The Future

Count your rainbows, not your storms.

- Karen K Sandhu

Chapter Twenty-five

Being body-confident

A conversation I had after having cervical cancer always sticks in my mind: after my fitness class one evening, I was talking with two ladies. One of them said she wasn't happy with the weight she carried on her hips. The other said she hated her stretch marks. Now, I could see a lady with great curves, and another with lines from growing her beautiful children. I showed the ladies my seven-inch scar from having cancer. They looked astonished. As I've written about, after my surgery I did go through a time when I felt I was never going to have a flat tummy again, but now I accept that. It took me time; time to go within myself and understand that this is me now. And now I love my scar. I have life.

So to me, your scars are your story: love yourself and love who you are and always be body-confident. As women, we should never compare ourselves with each other. When you accept that this is you – that you're beautiful and unique – and when you check in with yourself every day and tell yourself that, your thoughts on how you look will shift and make you more body-confident. And when you shine within, you truly shine out.

Confidence-boosting affirmations

* I am strong.
* I am giving.
* I am loving.
* I am powerful.
* I have great energy.
* I am helpful.
* I am a good listener.
* I am a good friend.
* I am healthy.
* I am becoming a better me every day.

Chapter Twenty-six

My training

September 2006 was the year I started my fitness journey. It felt strange going back to school (or should I say college), but I really wanted to find something I'd enjoy doing. The course was for two days a week, gym level 2. Going back to learning took some willpower. I laugh as I write this, as one of my close friends always says, 'Gosh, Lyndsey, you have willpower, girl!'

We were only a small a number – ten of us, all over 25 years of age, the oldest being 40. I loved every minute of it; learning how the body works and how to set up and plan a gym workout with the equipment.

When I got the qualification, I then wanted to further my education. I felt alive with the learning – a new-found me. But the gym level 3 course was £600 and that was a lot of money, especially being a single parent. Then – yes! I was talking to my lecturer and she told me there was a job vacancy in the gym at the college. If I worked there lunchtimes and evenings, the college would fund my course.

I was on to a winner. I loved the gym and the people at the college. We all supported each other and, as I like to say, your vibe is your tribe!

Level 3 was more about the muscle groups and learning about the heart. I used to drive my kids crazy with constantly repeating the names of the muscle groups, like they were my daily mantras. I was so happy learning. It was my new-found love for sure.

When exam time came round in summer 2007, I was ready. Well, I thought I was ready. I knew all the muscles and groups, but then it came to the heart. I loved the heart. But two weeks later when I got my results, I found I'd failed on the heart by two marks. I was gutted. I felt my confidence had been knocked. I went on and on about it to my kids. But then I kicked my own ass and passed the second time.

I built up a great friendship with one of the teachers at the college. She was a fitness coordinator at a local fitness club. She put me through the ETM course and, as I'd come from a dancing background, I picked it up quickly. It's all about knowing how to dance to music beats and, yes, I passed. So, by the end of 2007, I was certified across the fitness field. My teacher got me an interview, I got the job and started working in the gym. And I loved it, connecting with different people from all walks of life. She asked me if I'd like to train in group exercise classes, so I said yes and went for it. From 2008 to 2012, I trained in four group ex programmes, which I now still teach.

March 2017 is when I started my home study for cognitive behavioural therapy and life performance coaching, NLP. Now this took willpower! I would set myself up two afternoons a week and push myself hard, learning all the big words. By 2018, I'd become certified in both.

Getting out of your own way!

You are you and there will only ever be one of you. That's what I tell myself. Whatever thoughts come into our heads, we can choose how we perceive them. Be present in the moment and know you've got this thing called life!

'Nothing is impossible, the word itself says "I'm possible"' – Audrey Hepburn. So get up and dance with a high level of energy. Your brain is a muscle. Use it, work it. Hang around with great people, speak affirmations and kick ass.

Adversity

Any unpleasant situation is never nice to deal with. If I talked about things in the past while they were going on, my heart would pound, my body would shake. I felt I couldn't breathe with the fear of what was going to happen to me; the unknown, the power of the control of this person. I would put my head in my hands and beg, 'Please, just leave me!' I'd scream and cry. But the moment I shut up, it would get less; the kicks, the punching would slow down.

Then there was the pain of the wounds; the cuts, the bruises, the mental scars. But if I'd chosen to give up, where would my life have gone? How would it have turned out? I had to make a choice for myself. I knew I had to grow as me, as a person, and to learn to be strong for myself first. Then I could be strong for my children. And as I grew, the fear was turning into strength. T used to say to me, 'You'll have to leave our hometown to get away from me,' and I believed him. But as the years went by, I realised this was just one person who had power over me. And having these conversations with myself and getting the support I needed daily gave me the strength to understand that with anything in life, it's the relationship you have with it that matters – from drugs to loving somebody. It's about setting the barriers up and having the willpower to be consistent with yourself and to take every day as a new day: to never stop working on yourself.

My message to you:

If you live in the past... you'll be depressed.

If you live in the future... you'll be anxious.

If you live in the present... you'll be at peace.

And know that what you feel, you can heal.

I've learnt that no matter what, you have to be strong for the sake of yourself. It does take time, being patient with yourself and practising self-worth and self-love. It's not easy, but with the right mindset you can achieve it. I've had a lot of healing, counselling and coaching to help me to arrive at the peaceful mindset I have today; to love the life I live, full of self-love and abundance.

Also, I know that a thought is just that – a thought. It's how we perceive it that matters. Is what we're thinking even true? Let it in, let it out – and just let it be. I call this 'mind-chatter'. You are your thoughts and what you create. So think positive thoughts and take action by gaining clarity in your life about where you want to be.

Chapter Twenty-seven

Self-care

This is about being gentle and consistent with how I speak to myself and treat myself, and how I treat and talk to others and doing this with empathy. It's important to be caring and understanding, and to listen to others. We all have our own journeys and live in our own thoughts. I say this, as how we talk to others really does affect our own mindsets, how we feel, and our vibe. I eat good foods as I believe our daily diet also has a big impact on how we think and feel. I pamper myself too, with hot baths and massages, and have relaxing time, switch-off time, just for me. I dress in clothes that make me feel like the woman I want to be: fitted dresses on special occasions, or gym wear when I'm working out. Either way, it's great to feel fantastic within. I have my make-up applied by a great friend, even just for days when I'm not going anywhere, because it makes me feel good. I take pride in myself, in my mind body and soul.

Gratitude and meditation are a must on my list: make them a must on yours too. I read books that inspire me, my first choice being *You Can Heal Your Life* by Louise

Hay. What an inspiring lady, God rest her soul. I also still love dancing. It's an amazing feeling to get your energy flowing and I highly recommend you give it a go. Energy goes where energy flows: everything is energy, from how we vibe to how it makes us feel.

I meditate too. I find it calms me down, bringing me to where I am in the moment. I sit up with my back straight, cross my legs, relax my arms with the palms of my hands facing upwards, and I'm open to the universe. I breathe in through my nose right into my stomach, and straight out again through my nose. I have my thoughts clear in my head and, whatever I want to manifest in my life, I focus on that. I let it in and let it out through just being, and I always bring myself back to my breath again and just being present in the moment.

I do have my days when I'm not feeling 100 per cent too, and I allow these days. I accept them and just stay grounded in the moment.

Chapter Twenty-eight

Miracle mornings!

How I start my day

I always have water at the side of my bed so when I wake up, I can drink it. I get up, stretch and make my bed, and then I meditate. I have a book called *A Deep Breath Of Life,* written by Alan Cohen, who is also the author of *A Course In Miracles*, and it has daily inspirations. I always seem able to relate the daily inspiration to my life – the universe knows. I read the one for my day and get that good vibe of self-inspiration to start my morning.

I then make my breakfast shake, which is spinach, banana, an orange, blueberries, celery, chia seeds, coconut water and protein powder before I get the tunes on and do my workout. After that, my mind and body are ready to take on the day.

My rule in the morning is no TV at all and I only check my phone for emails and messages after I've had my time to get ready for the day ahead. How you start your day has such an impact on how it will turn out. So get yourself into a routine of greatness for you, as we really are 80 per cent mindset and 20 per cent physiology. That makes you think, doesn't it?

I'll be honest, there are the days when I have a great night out with the girls and a good few drinks, and I lie in my bed the next morning, craving water and a bacon sandwich. And I give myself permission for those days, when the TV is on and I can hang out with a good Netflix show and just chill. It really is about living with balance and it's the key.

Think about this:

* Is it your intention to build a life you love right now?

* Are you ready to step into the best, higher version of yourself?

* Do you want to learn the difference between self-worth and confidence, and fully implement them – knowing that you are the badass you truly are?

Then take this action – and watch your life shift and change.

Conclusion

So, this was my story: raw and real. My journey. If I can leave you with anything, it's to know that you are your own superhero and you've got this!

Be consistent in everything you do every day and be grateful for what you have. Write down your gratitude list: start with ten things you're really grateful for, then add more each day. Create affirmations that say what you want them to, and repeat them 20 times a day. Be clear with your affirmations. If it's a new job you want, state what the job is and write it down 20 times. Have a good relationship with money and know that everything is coming to you in abundance in your life.

Here are my top ten must-do things that I do for me, and would love you to do for you too:

1. Have gratitude.

2. Journal.

3. Create and repeat affirmations.

4. Eat healthily.

5. Drink plenty of water.

6. Meditate.

7. Exercise.

8. Pamper yourself.

9. Vibe high with your tribe.

10. Love yourself first.

And visualise! Get yourself a vision board. Cut pictures out of magazines of your dream house, job, car, family – everything that your heart truly desires – and stick them to the board. Get them out there to the universe and believe in the law of attraction: see it, live it, feel it, get super excited about it all. I repeat: live it, believe it, dream it, achieve it.

Get out of your comfort zone! Do scary things that test you but make you feel alive inside!

My message to you:

Every time you feel pain, know deep down that you have a purpose in this world. Love yourself for who you are and live the life that was planned for you. Every fear, every pain that you have ever felt is what has made you the person you are. Every person and everything that is still with you

is as it is supposed to be: your life, your journey, because you are love.

Everyone else has their own journey. So focus on you and those close to you. Never fear – you've got this. Be your own super power. The world needs you to show up being the best you can ever be.

Be bold. Be brave. Be beautiful. Be you.

Take that leap of faith.

Have willpower and:

* Replace bad habits with good habits.

* Have the courage to change your life; to rewrite your story.

* Connect with great people who improve your life.

* Clear your mind, check in with the present, put your hand on your heart, and breathe.

* Hang out with people that kick your ass – ditch the blood-suckers.

* Use your mind – it's a powerful muscle – and set your goals.

* Write your goals down.

* Dream them and believe them.

* Post notes of them everywhere.

* Affirm them and love your journey.

My mission

I am here to serve every single person who needs me to show up for them. I want you to know that you are amazing and powerful; that you're beautiful, inside and out. You are living your own life and time isn't just passing you by. When I look back at what I've learnt in life and how I've been told I have a story, a gift to pass on through my great energy – this is all for you. Life really is about you, and loving you... and by taking these little steps, you will be the creator of your own amazing life.

As I sit here writing this, it's the 17th April 2020. The world is gripped by a pandemic –the Covid-19 virus. With so much of life shut down, this has given me the time to write and to finish this book. I hope it's shown you that there is power in each one of us to transform ourselves into who we want to be and to have the life we deserve to have. You just have to show up, do the work, and love yourself first.

I now have four beautiful grandchildren as well as my three wonderful children. They are all such amazing souls with fantastic futures ahead of them. I live in a village, in a home I love. There are fields for miles and horses pass by every day. Life really could never be better for me.

We grow as people every day and we are always learning about ourselves. I'll say it again: just don't forget to love yourself first.

Before I started my personal development journey, I saw a quote on Instagram:

'How do you know that you were meant to be a healer?'

'Because I kept falling in love with broken people.'

'Then why are you alone?'

'Because I am broken too. So I am falling in love with myself first to get a taste of my own medicine...'

I now call myself a 'recovery coach' as I truly believe we can all recover from absolutely anything in life. We just have to want it, and to know that everything we want in life is on the way to us.

You can get in touch and connect with me anytime:

Email: Lyndsey_austin@yahoo.co.uk

Website: LyndseyAustinlifecoach.com

Facebook: Lyndsey Austin

Instagram: Lyndsey_Austin /#flightofabutterfly

Twitter: Lyndsey Austin @lyndz30

LinkedIn: Lyndsey Austin

Every moment there is a choice. A choice to think a new thought, a decision to create a new feeling, a chance to make a new reality. Take it!

- Lyndsey Austin

Acknowledgements

There are so many people I want to thank.

First, my children, for listening and understanding why I wanted to publish a book telling about my journey, and for understanding too that my pain was my gain, and my path is to serve and help others in their lives.

Secondly, to Karen K. Sandha, who gave me the beautiful, inspirational quotes dotted through the book; Rikki Miles for helping me create the page to publish my book and also a big thank you to Alexa (and her team) from The Book Refinery who turned my Word document into the beautiful pages you see here.

And then, there are all my friends – I have so many, which is amazing! Your vibe is your tribe and I want to thank every single one of you for all the great times we've had and for the support you've all given me.

And finally, I want to thank my coaches, who have pushed me to be the coach I am today. All you guys rock!

Printed in Great Britain
by Amazon

55700993R00077